# SHARP GOLDEN THORN

# SHARP GOLDEN THORN
## POEMS BY CHARD DENIORD

For Eric and Tamara,

Chard
5/20/15

MARSH HAWK PRESS | NEW YORK | 2003

FIRST EDITION

03 04 05 7 6 5 4 3 2 1

Marsh Hawk Press books are published by Poetry Mailing List, Inc., a not-for-profit corporation under United States Internal Revenue Code.

COVER DESIGN: Brian Cohen and Soren deNiord
AUTHOR PHOTO: Pete Gunther
BOOK DESIGN: Rayna deNiord

I am greatful to the following people for their support and valuable suggestions in helping me to shape this book: Liz deNiord, Soren deNiord, Eric Rawson, Heather McHugh, Thomas Lux, Philip Levine, Jeff Friedman, Bruce Smith, Jacqueline Gens, Anne Marie Macari, Brian Cohen, Dave Calicchio, Ethan Canin, Tony Sanders and Peter Johnson. I would especially like to thank Rayna deNiord for her skill and effort in designing this book.

Printed in the United States by McNaughton & Gunn

Library of Congress Cataloging-in-Publication Data

DeNiord, Chard, 1952 -
Sharp golden thorn: poems / by Chard deNiord
    p. cm.
ISBN 0-9724785-3-1
I. Title
PS3554.E532S53 2003
811'.54--dc22

                                              2003014984

MARSH HAWK PRESS
PO Box 220, Stuyvesant Station
New York, New York 10009

marshhawkpress.org

FOR GERRY

# ACKNOWLEDGEMENTS

**ANTHOLOGIES**

Best American Poetry, 1999: "What The "Animals Teach Us"
Pushcart Prize, 1998: "Pasternak"

**JOURNALS**

New England Review: "Pasternak," "The Book Of Darkness," "Silver Shrine"

Agni: "Last Date," "Descent," "Revival"

Ploughshares: "Burning the Brush," "The Invisible Body," "A Glimpse of the Afterlife," "Harold Bloom," "The Soul As A Body," "Last Song"

Harvard Review: "Dream Of A New World Order," "What The Animals Teach Us," "Abelard In Ecstasy," "Error At The Heart Of Desire" under the title "On The Mountain Of Spices," "Goshawk"

Harvard Magazine: "Like A Shadow At Evening"

The American Voice: "The Sadness of Daughters"

Metropolitan Review: "An Extraordinary Evening In Providence"

Greensboro Review: "The Worms"

Kenyon Review: "Crow"

The Antioch Review: "The Belle Of Amherst"

The Denver Quarterly: "Sharp Golden Thorn," "In My Estrangement," "Acheron"

Crazyhorse: "Elegy For A Dress," "Epitaph"

River Styx: "Is Sex A Soiled Gown"
Green Mountains Review: "Aubade For A Convert"
The Bad Henry Review: "In The Privacy Of Our
    Bedroom"
North Dakota Quarterly: "The Crippling Field"
Witness: "Every Imagination"
Quarterly West: "Birder"
Pequod: "Lilith"
Graham House Review: "Transubstantiation"
The Mississippi Review: "The Flashing Zone"
Northwest Review: "The Rain As Rain
The Iowa Review: "The Bailiff Of The Heavenly Court Brings
    Gerry To The Lord's Attention,""Comfort Crow"
Smartish Pace: "The Greater Vision"
The Alembic: "Winter Roses"
For Poetry: "Judith"

Love pierced my heart
with its thorn.
One day I got it out-
now the heart is numb...
My song laments once more.
Sharp golden thorn
if only I could feel you
piercing my heart.

ANTONIO MACHADO


I carried inside me a cut and bleeding soul, and how
to get rid of it I just didn't know. For where could my
heart flee from my heart? Where could I escape
myself?

ST. AUGUSTINE

# TABLE OF CONTENTS

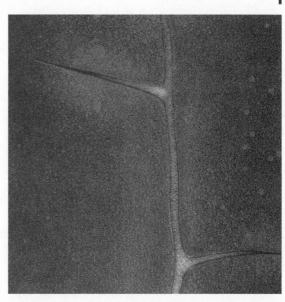

# IN MY ESTRANGEMENT

## BURNING THE BRUSH

I knew a force lay hidden in the air
that could raise this heat from only a spark,
lick the sky and still be hungry.
I lit a page of rolled up news and ran
out back with arm upraised and stuck
it under. It didn't catch at first.
I threw a cup of diesel on, and then
another, until a plume of smoke, blue
with rain, billowed up from the center.
A hemlock flared and crackled at the needles.
A birch burned down like a cigarette.
I stared at the fire that had formed a heart
and tongue together and raged in rain.
I watched it rise like a beautiful dress.
I imagined putting it on, a new garment
for this moment only put out by the next.
I'd wear it at death and submit
my soul as a body that burned like this.
I fell asleep open-eyed and dreamed of fire.
I heard a coal insist, *Spread this fashion
of fiery dress across the land. Rise up
from here to your beloved. Burn forever.*

## SHARP GOLDEN THORN

I loved the feel of your mouth against mine.
I loved the sight of your body next to me.
I said to you while you slept,
"Look what God has made."
My eyes grew ten thousand lids in my sleep.
When the sun came up I opened them all all morning
onto the sight of you.
I was both myself and a host of witnesses.
I thought, What would I do without you?
How could my memory sustain me?
How could this thorn remain inside me?
I was remembering and watching you at the same time.
I was dying and becoming inside the flames.
I was the man in the fire that is his beloved.

## ALL NIGHT

She worked with the dust
until she *came to Her*, walking
on the water, falling in place
beneath the light of a lesser light.

She laid her down like a corpse
and breathed in her a single breath
that tripped her heart with a beat.
She was good like everything else
already created. She fell asleep
one night and dreamed of herself
in another form: her, yet not her, a man.

He was both logical *and* absurd.
He was the Lord's embarrassed answer.

She dreamed of him throughout the night
and then awoke to find him there, asleep,
dreaming himself of who knows what.
She tried to guess. Already *another?*
She slapped his cheeks and pinched his arm.
She kissed his lips and straddled his back.

"You must start again in reverse,"
she said to Her, "or make him dream of me.
He thinks that he must give unearthly birth to me.
That he alone must name the animals.
This is the beginning you must create
to make him see that I came first.

## ABELARD IN ECSTASY

You swam like a snake with your head outstretched above
the water. I cut a wake inside your wake
and followed you into the shallows. We stood
in a tight embrace, sinking down in the leafy muck,
holding on as if we'd break on letting go.
A single cloud in the shape of a horse galloped past
on his way to the barn. I saw the sky for what it was,
immaculate field, burial ground. A voice called out
from the other side, "Heloise! Abelard!" The voice
of your uncle carrying far across the water for us to return.
We were surrounded by a thousand minnows
with shiny badges. I couldn't speak as I looked
at you and saw myself refracted there, so deep in bliss,
so damn ecstatic, the world was bent for good.
I heard my voice when you responded, "Coming, uncle!"
We swam ashore and dressed in vain. The darkness
fell inside the light as I rowed us back to the Christian world.

## ELEGY FOR A DRESS

She wore it once then hung it up,
telling herself that she was happy enough without it,
that to ask for anything more would be a dangerous prayer
that God might answer.
She was afraid that she would burn if she left it on,
although the tag specifically said
that it would burn if it wasn't worn.
All those years she was turning heads
with older garments from the newest stores
the forgotten dress smoldered inside her closet
like a fire that burns in water,
like a ghost trapped on a hanger.
It was her raiment that needed her body to keep its form.
To burn on her in the highest fashion.

# AN EXTRAORDINARY EVENING IN PROVIDENCE


I looked down on the city from a cloud
as if I were dead but still alive somehow
and saw the fires burning in a row of floating cauldrons
in the new canal of Providence.
The moon was full as tens of thousands filled the streets
to witness the spectacle of floating fires.
To stare at the water as dark as night.
There was music also-Italian songs-that hung
on the surface, then rose to the sky
where the stars shone down like sparks
from the fires, still burning, burning.
We were so strange in the crowd
as children paddled around the cauldrons
and people greeted each other like souls.
I stood on a bridge suspended now
by more than stones and watched myself pass below
as someone else in the bow of a black gondola.
She said, *Belief is a committee that doesn't meet*
to the man beside her who wanted to kiss.
She said, *The old world is new when you remember*
*the dead and all they did to outdo themselves.*
I was in love with myself in the form of her
on the river of fire. The sky was a face
with only eyes, and I was blind.
She entered the darkness under the bridge
as if she were reading between the stars.
I was forgetting and remembering at the same time.
I was fueling the fires burning my mind.

# DREAM OF A NEW WORLD ORDER

We're in bed beneath a goose down quilt
in the dacha of a friend who can't return.
Painted eggs adorn the sill.
The stove is packed with birch on low.
It is December and for the first time in seventy years
there are lights in the windows again.
We are watching the end
of Eisenstein's *Bezhin Meadow* on the VCR,
corrupted by its formalism of purple flowers.

It's snowing again.

We discuss the movie's *poetry* for a while,
the indelible, disparate things that contradict
the state's denial of the soul.
You say, "This country roamed the ward for seventy
years stabbing its heart with a German blade."
You say, "Now showing on the giant screen
of the fallen world the censored film of a meadow."

We get up for dinner in our robes
and have some caviar, borscht and wine.
We put *Gorky* on and lie back down.
Your father calls.
You spill your wine on my pillow reaching for the phone.
You ask him how he got our number.
"Never mind," he says, "now listen..."

You tell him that you're with me now,
that communism is dead, that without the example of love
both here and at home the world is doomed.

He tells you that love is a criminal roaming your heart
with a golden tongue, that the world never changes
despite the end of empires and the hopes of the young.
I can hear his American voice in the Russian receiver:
"What about those folks in the permafrost just north of you?
What about Mandelstam, Sakharov and Wallenberg?
Tell me one damned thing their love did for them."
You tell him about the baby then.
He falls as silent as the snow.
We are at the part where Gorky is walking
beside the Volga, taking it in, seeing who he is.
The snow is melting in the fields.
The sun is out and the ice is breaking.

I take the phone from you as Gorky stares at the scud
of floes and I tell your father that he'll be sorry
if he thinks "America" can happen in a country
where the sausages are filled with sawdust
and the vodka bottles have no caps, where the ghosts
of ten thousand peasants cry out from the ground like stones
and all the officials are in love with difficulty,
where madness, passion and nihilism tour the countryside
in a dazzling troika, and a nose absconds
to a stranger's oven, where the songs are funny,
long and sad and everyone votes for the common man.
I tell him this is the right place for love,
so error-ridden and cold,
that we may be here forever, this far removed,
somewhere in Siberia, watching films about meadows

and the children who survived the war,
learning the language slowly, one difficult word at a time.
I say good bye and hang up the phone.

An old man down the road without any teeth
utters a proverb from the time of Rus:
"Eat bread and salt and speak the truth."
The camera closes in on his face.
It has that unabashed, mystified Russian look
that burns the script.
He is catching the backside of the Lord.
I kiss your neck as you fall asleep.
It's 1914. It's 2001.

# THE SADNESS OF DAUGHTERS

She polished the oak of her father's floor
with her hair. Her beauty grew as she progressed
with the terrible fear that she was bleeding
from a wound inside, perhaps to death.
Her blood ran down her leg and onto the floor.
She fled the house to the gravity spring
in the upper field. Studied herself
in the rebus there. The face she saw
on the surface glare deferred to a depth.
Bright stare of things on the bottom where
her face transfigured to leaves, stone
and flower. Surprise. The self that shines
as other through the lens of water.
Now the flower would give her away.
Sing the syllable of seeing
beyond the mirror. Her father inquired
about the blood when she returned.
Stood silent at the door when she replied,
"There is no cure for the life inside."

## LAST SONG

You sang to me throughout the winter
the same desultory song.
Each flake of snow, each pellet of ice
fell like music to the frozen ground.
I lived on crackers in a cardboard house.
Got down on my knees and sang to the dirt,
"Go ahead, my dear.
Eat all *his* fruit this year.
Each seed you swallow doubles your beauty.
Chills your heart."

# IN THE PRIVACY OF OUR BEDROOM

We think about trees and their demands
on the wind, how they stand in such
tranquility outside the window
and change the light to air.

We watch the sun deceive our sense
of stillness and wonder now, too late,
why we say the sun is setting
when *we* are turning toward the stars.

We grow close to the dark
like things put away and turn down
the sheet and climb inside
like a word for sleep to spell.

We know our psalm without waking up,
the line that repeats itself:
"Your hurt is incurable,
and your wound is grievous."

We forget the dream that frightened us
and fuse ourselves for now and now again.
We wake at two and think it's dawn
and rise like ghosts to haunt ourselves.

## SILVER SHRINE

I was inventing a tree
on the train, forgetting distance,
listening to the wheels, gazing
at the scenery like a chimpanzee
in his cage. I was far enough
above the ground to think
about gravity and all the other
technicalities that hold me down.
I was streaming along,
putting my mind to higher things.
I was imagining the engineer as *her,*
my antelope, my pomegranate, my beautiful analyst.
I reclined with an automatic hand
and wrote this down extinguished,
as if it had already been written
and I was just remembering it
like a soul with a sudden body in transit
across New Jersey: first leather,
then steel, then carpet.

I was devout among these chairs
taking leave of my seat, while staying seated.
What did I see?
A train with me on it and the others
that I adored for their proximity
and startling resemblance.

"Honesty is less the issue
than the lies you choose to endure."
I was making it up: there is a law
to forgetfulness which we obey perforce.
The driver is anonymous and mute.

You are surprised to see yourself
behind the gate. "Pass by. Pass by," he says
when the curtain falls of its own accord
and you head into the country of a half-familiar world.

This was my grief in wakefulness:
the overheard confession across the aisle:
"I have yet to learn my purpose in life."
I was reminded of Habakkuk on the run,
an irresistible antithesis: his quickness at moving on.
Although I was not catching up to where
I might have been in glorious flames without a burn,
I was catching on for a moment.
I was trusting *her* to switch the tracks responsibly,
and I was coming to the awareness
of time's invention which led me next
to think of space and movement
and the theory of change: Create
the situation of motion in motion
for a brilliant passenger and something happens
that causes her to ask, "Will we ever get there?
What if I took a train on the train on the train?
Would the mullions disappear and the scenery blur
and the station extend from here to there?
Would it be possible to enter the door
at the end of the aisle?"

I grew dizzy and turned to the woman beside me.
I put on the same defeated face as the man
across the aisle. I loved him now that I was he.
She told me her name and the company
to which she was applying.

She brought me around to where
the earth stopped spinning.
It was 2003 somewhere in New Jersey
and the war was on.

"Sometimes I worry that love is not enough," she pined.
"Augustine was wrong," I said,
to think that the things of this world
have fallen, that our awareness changed
the earth, that everything dies like us.
Look at that tank and tenement house.
Think of the turtle with her head
for distance and her heart for roads.
Who is a genius at logarithms and greeter of wind."

My head began to spin again.
I didn't know what to think in the wake of the passing world
that faded on a wave of fields and marsh:
What is the code on the turtle's shell?
Am *I* ready to bless what I cannot spell?
I made this start in the Meadowlands:
Bless this time it takes to bless.
Bless my seat of helplessness.
Bless this rail across the earth.
Bless this train that passes by.

## IN MY ESTRANGEMENT

I held an inquiry in my heart.
It said it could not wait for me to see
what it had seen already.
It said that I was at its mercy
when I least expected.
It spoke with a terrible confidence
about its lot, how since it was trapped
it thought of others behind my back.
In everything else, it said, you are irregular.
I demand this sacrifice for my consistency.
Convict me if you wish.
Make it official for the stupid judge.
Each day you live I leave unfinished.
I saw the *face of death* in another woman.
She glanced at me and I responded.
*I was thinking of nothing else*
but how to go on living.
If I apologize for this
you won't believe me.

## EVERY IMAGINATION

I kissed your ribs and feet.
"Later," you said.
"Let's get some sleep."
I turned on the lamp and read Tacitus to you,
his lucid account of Nero's plot to kill his mother.
"Strike here!" she begged, pointing to her womb.

"Can you imagine?" you said.
"Her very own son.
Now turn off the light."

"Yes, yes, he was mad.
He imbibed from night's well.
The entire Roman Empire was at his mercy,
which didn't exist."

I straddled you like a crane
and kissed your neck.
It was both early and late.
"Which is the norm?" I asked.
"Goodness or evil?"
You frowned in your sleep.
"Not enough sugar."

"Evil," I said.
"In every imagination."

We are the children of Agrippina.

I kissed your shoulders and smelled your hair.
It smelled like the willows of heaven.
I kissed your forehead, eyes and ears.
"Strike here," I said. "Strike here."

## LILITH

I didn't move but lay outstretched.
"Think of something else," she said.
I felt the sky upon my wrists.
"I'm that and that condensed as this."

She breathed on me with perfumed breath.
She kissed my knees with purple lips.
I had awakened to her naked-
ness. "You are the one I've missed,"

I said, "who came to me in dreams.
Forgive this sleep that runs its course,
that greets its dream in weariness."
She took my hand with tenderness

and rested it between her legs.
I felt the clouds break into me
like thieves. I was afraid but stirred
as I lay on her like a god who's died.

I pressed my lips against her breasts.
The animals fled to the wilderness.

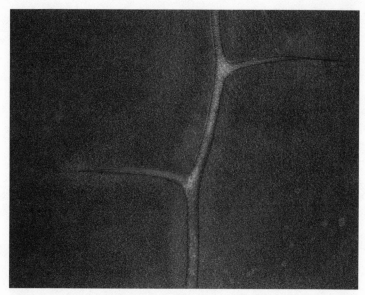

# EVERY BRILLIANT CREATURE

# WHAT THE ANIMALS TEACH US

that love is dependent on memory,
that life is eternal and therefore criminal,
that thought is an invisible veil that covers our eyes,
that death is only another animal,
that beauty is formed by desperation,
that sex is solely a human problem,
that pets are wild in heaven,
that sounds and smells escape us,
that there are bones in the earth without any marker,
that language refers to too many things,
that music hints at what we heard before we sang,
that the circle is loaded,
that nothing we know by forgetting is sacred,
that humor charges the smallest things,
that the gods *are* animals without their masks,
that stones tell secrets to the wildest creatures,
that nature is an idea and not a place,
that our bodies have diminished in size and strength,
that our faces are terrible,
that our eyes are double when gazed upon,
that snakes do talk, as well as asses,
that we compose our only audience,
that we are geniuses when we wish to kill,
that we are naked despite our clothes,
that our minds are bodies in another world.

## THE SOUL AS A BODY

There's a body inside the body.
It's the form that rises up, immune
to fire. It's the kingdom of nothing
as a body. High nothing! You see
its shell in the mirror, draw back.
Feel ashamed. It wakes in a dream
and speaks in silence. Suffers names.
What do you call it? The one as two?
Grain of salt? Eater of seeds?
Behold its raiment as it transfigures.
A threadless garment-force as form.
Fatal shroud. You cannot touch it.
It rises from your groin like a quail
with vertical power. Leaps like a trout
to catch the fly in an arc that spans
the world. There is a medium inside
the body like water or air in which
this other body swims, is quick to
disappear, you, yet not you. Each creature
a surprise of need's design. Each need
determined by another need until
there's only light. The more you dress
it up in a single form the less you see
what you cannot see at first. The less
you know the multitudes inside you.
It is a body that has come to you
with a passionate love. That sees itself
in all things. That cannot live without you.

## CROW

I awoke this morning to the rumbling sound
of a crow rolling a bone on the flat-top roof
outside my window.
From her routine
rounds above the house this genius saw
that I was sleeping, at least not moving,
behind the screen.
Safe for the time being,
long enough for touching down and picking
the joint's luscious marrow.
Such a gutsy
hungry bird with a constant smile that said,
"Did you hear the one about the man in an open
field?"
"No," I said inside my dream,
because I was also dreaming this.
She never
told the answer, as if this funny answer
were plain enough to every brilliant creature.
The sound of laughter filled the trees across
the yard.
She risked her life for a taste of fat.
"But oh what a taste!" she cawed to the ranks
of other crows on lofty branches.
"Oh taste and see!"
No murder this morning across the sky but early
waking to a clown in love with a bone.
She waited
for my lids to cock my eyes without a click,
then blink, and when they did she raised her wings
in flight to speak, "He isn't real you know."

## THE INVISIBLE BODY

I imagined every creature before I spoke
with fatal names. You were the leopard and goat.
You were the kestral and loon.
I had the power of speech because of you.
Ten thousand things came into being
from a single form that was not a form.
I made no sense like this in the after language
to name the animals. I asked your help
with the flowers, some small relief
from too many things, some purple Latin
to quiet their blossoms. I stared at you at dawn
with a look that opened doors onto a door
that had no room, a hardened glass
through which I saw the same new world
where I was dumb and good but not yet strange.

# BIRDER

You see everything from a distance as if it were near;
this is my only complaint: what you imagine
is accurate enough but hardly true.
This goldfinch, for instance, is not a thrush,
although both birds do frequent the feeder.
Oh, lonesome seer of the hillock,
do you not see how active the maids are
in their various bowers?
What can I tell you? Yes, the same old sunflowers
attract your favorite cynosures.
Yes, that glint of yellow is endowed with ancient song.
But now I'm telling you like a voice amidst the crowd
that a knight of faith, a post woman, is listening
from afar as if her life depended on it.
Just as the man at the bar isn't really sorry
for bumping the waitress, you see things
that are hypothetical in order to sing, in order to live.
Don't let all the antinomy fool you, that is,
the millennial palaver. It's so much elliptical tinder.
So much love talk. Do you hear it?
Brother, I am afraid. This mercy has lasted
way too long, not for the birds, God bless them,
but for us. No genius, of which there is plenty,
convinces me in the valley that nothing is good,
that blue is black, that the thrush is deaf.

## ROMANCE

I swim  like a turtle in the city pool,
slow deliberate laps, like a body
in space whose speed is relative,
both fast and slow, fast for here
where a tension binds a thing
to space, as if a space were not
a void but a possible place for
a thing to be.
                        Any movement,
therefore, the slightest quake,
is lightning quick, but for the thing
in space denied by distance and
everything else, speed is fiction,
a figure on a dial that needs a wheel,
till something nears, still
for centuries, and passes by.
                                    I see
you in the pool as just such a body,
still in the void I fill with the water,
although the water is already there.
(The void remains despite the water.)
This is the double life of water, there
and there again when someone's in it,
for it's not itself when left alone.
I imagine breathing inside the water
where  an absence of strata weds
the air to a molecule that turns
a hole into a pool.

        I am laughing
at the hare ahead of time, deferring
to a darkness that makes a point.
I am breathing hard like a pilgrim
who suffers for what he believes:
the removal of words, the illusion
of speed.
        I am breathing hard
from fearing the distance from here
to there.
        Because I cannot exist
just here, because I cannot help
imagining you as a body in space,
as a star, I must imagine the place
that ceases to be, this pool,
where I am cancelled by nothing,
where I am free in a kind of grace
that denies itself, that simply is,
that is finally nothing.
                    There is
the dance that no one can see out there,
where the serpent sleeps and the blackbird sings,
where the body moves to make us blind.

# THE WORMS

My wife's stirring the worms in the basement.
I'm upstairs boiling water for the hydroculator.
The dead fox my son brought in last fall from the road
still lies beneath the snow on top of the shed
that I fell off of last week, injuring my back.
I call the old boy Polyneices one day and Eteocles the next.
I'm tempting fate, I know, but what's worse, getting hit
by a truck crossing the street on your way to church
or living each day gripping a brooch?

Each day I climb up to see what the air has wrought.
Still whole in the cold, perfectly preserved.
I leave him be as long as he smiles,
as long as his lips still cling to his bones.

The red wrigglers roil in the green wormorium.
The tea pot whistles its single note.
I stand transfixed at the kitchen sink
staring out the window at the snowy field.
A crow flies by like a pair of scissors, cutting
the world into everything and nothing.
A fox appears at the edge of the yard, then runs away.
I smile slowly to keep the sky from cracking.

## GOSHAWK

How many times have I told this story?
There I was ambling along in search of dessert
inside the orchard when a goshawk dove on me
with outstretched talons.

There I was all dressed in cotton
in the cool of evening, inspecting
the trees for infestation,
when a goshawk harrowed me.

There I was pinned to the ground
like a reprobate with my liver exposed
as a fresh hors d'oeuvre on a dusty plate
when a goshawk circled me in figure eights.

There I was crawling away
behind the trees where the apples hung
like brains, and nothing I said
reminded this bird of who I was.

## ELEPHANT

I stood and waited in an open field
for the great mahout. He went to work
on my back, weighing me down with sacks.
I screamed until my voice gave out.
Fell to my knees beneath the weight of a straw.
In time, I learned to understand his voice:
"Forget your past. Live this life. The long way out
has no way back." He taught me things
that made me strange. How to pick him up
with my trunk and wave. How to genuflect
to the crowd. I had my nature but no more will.
I felt a bone inside my memory break.

# THE FLASHING ZONE

I have cast out the sky
and see the day again that everyone sees.
It is a hungry carp that bites each time.
What to do with all these fish
that lie on the counter and stink?
Where are the hungry when you need them?

I want you in moderation.
I want you when I cannot have you.
I want you in this and the other world.
I want you to call me your dolphin
who swims from here to there through the swells,
who lives with the sea by leaping from it,
who once thought the ocean formless,
who concedes to form for the sake of swimming,
who craves the feel of water around him,
who desires you, like the ocean for swimming,
who stitches the waves in joy and fitness and equilibrium.

The lights are flashing again.
This beauty in the eye of the dying beholder
is a rail, is emptiness, is form.
A blinking angel says that this is the cure
for the body born too soon.

## LIKE A SHADOW AT EVENING

I am content to open my chair
in the Indian air and sit like an owl
above the world reciting psalms
that curse the enemy. It is October.
I eulogize each falling leaf: signs
of something greater, a realm of life
beyond my grief, amusement on every corner.
I am absurd with this belief.
My darkness is the angels' mirror.
What do they see? Nothing at first,
then a wrinkled face they call their own
for both our sakes. How should I fly?
By falling and turning?
By not thinking of landing?
By knowing the dream of sleep?
I sit on my lap like a child and pinch my leg.
*I am gone, like a shadow at evening.*
*I am shaken off like a locust.*

## THE VOID WAS YOURS


I embraced you like an atmosphere.
How to wake you without waking you?
I held your breasts like passion fruit.
You were a country at peace
with your back to the world.
I swam in the river of your back.
Dove down to the loam of your floor.
How to remain the bear?
How to face you from behind?
I kissed your neck to make you turn.
I shot the rapids of your spine.
What did you see as you faced away?
The void was yours instead of mine.

## THE BLUES

I felt their fins against my shins
as I stood transfixed in the ocean.
I regarded them as souls for whom
the water was the dream of their bodies
come true, whose hunger burned
inside the sea as a cold blue flame.
I prayed for them to hear my prayer
of permitting me to go on praying
my same great prayer. I rubbed
the water that they had burned
to ash all over me, until it cooled.

## I STOOD NAKED

in the frozen field below the house.
Time dressed in darkness.
I sang a silly song about me and my shadow.
A crow flew overhead, landed on my shoulder.
He was my priest without a collar,
the right hand of nature.
I uncrossed myself and smelled the snow.
There was no forgiveness.
My heart glittered from above like tinsel.
Turned dull as stone on earth.

## AUBADE FOR A CONVERT

Take a stone, any stone, and see what a gem
it becomes in your hand. All things are like
this stone, hidden in their obvious places,
opal, diamond, sapphire, always waiting
with eternal patience for us to become
that thing we say it is-stone, flower, tree.
There is always something in the dark, my dear.
You can hear it fluttering at the top of the trees.
It's the cage that kills in the end. Leave the door open
now for the curious sparrow. Already its song
is an adequate theme for anyone who listens.
Already the world is barred when it escapes.

III

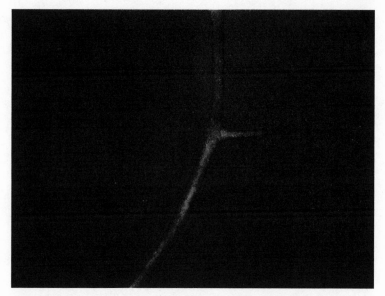

# FLIGHT DELAY AT TERMINAL X

# TRANSUBSTANTIATION

I said yes immediately when you asked if I believed
in it   and I didn't feel that foolish for saying so
although I did feel foolish afterwards in thinking
about it   for there was nothing I could say to prove it
I only knew that it was true in another way that made
religious sense   in *linking back* to a metaphor that kept
its word   that loved the body as well as mind and took
another form by which we came to call something else
the blood and body of Christ   fully conscious then
of the difference between the *substitute* and flesh itself
which was so mutable in his duress that vanity proposed
to death   and fruit transformed from words to flesh
or else His voice lacked the strength to bear a hazelnut
from nothingness   the taste of *it* quite moot as long
as we believe   lives in us in such a way that we could say
with confidence that this was that and that was this because
he said it was and what he said was not a metaphor in the way
we think   in curious ways that made us feel and see anew
and think again   but not believe in bleeding bread
I mean my love *was* the rose of Sharon but only because
she inspired this while staying herself and knowing
the difference   hearts were prone to such fallaciousness
yet when we said *we take this bread* our hearts were seized
by what was possible   which was *all things* but not everything
you see   which was absurd and mystical   which was
the Paraclete becoming a meal and entering *our* bodies
like an idea   but not an idea since the host was form
already   and fusing him with us in prayer   but only then
when we were ready and knew the presence of his body as real
if changed for a while   for the sake of becoming him

## LAST DATE

I was a walking dead man
with my beloved at my side.
I turned to her and smiled
from the other world.
We were on our way to the Cafe Raou.
I was granted this last walk
by the Lord of the Underworld.
He was not offended by the happiness
of two lovers walking hand in hand
for one last time.
This was his blessing that I desired.
I said something forgettable
as we crossed the street.
She laughed at whatever it was
and held me tighter.
I was all soul.
I had no witnesses besides the other lovers.
We formed a chorus outside the cafe
and sang, "You are my sunshine, my only sunshine."
I ordered a decaf with vanilla
and a little whip cream.
We sat at on the terrace and observed
the clouds destroy themselves.
I saw myself moving my lips
and holding her hand.
I was telling her I loved her again
for the ten thousandth time.
I took a sip of coffee and watched
my skin turn pale.
I had agreed to this condition
in order to return: unname the flowers,
keep turning around.

## LOVE LETTER

It's not that the moment when I see someone
for who she is couldn't exist at some other time.
It could; that's not the point.
It's the world at that moment coming to me
like a friend who has dissolved into things like Vasudeva,
corrected my vision in a way that allows me to see
how closely connected I am to whatever happens,
no matter how distant-a twister in Kansas, a draft in Paris.
That the world is dependent on me and you
for defining things, that this is why we're here,
for the sake of knowing is all, since without us
there would be no apprehension as we know it,
which is what we want to confess to something
greater than ourselves, such as a tree or buffalo or stone.
For how can we be enough in the end to ourselves?
Bear these burdens of error?

What we think, know and feel is already inherent
in the world but too much a part of it.
Untranslated. Blessed.
The sky makes fun of us in its mirror
if we can't say to ourselves,
*You old mute sky,*
*we are the masters of non sequiturs.*
*Do with us what you will.*

This sort of talk is for our own benefit,
religious by default, sacrilege by necessity.
I say to you, *You're a little walking temple.*
*So sacred with all that sovereignty, freedom and power.*

We must all have a liturgy for ourselves.
I'll begin mine by saying
that everything I say about me I say also about you.
Forgive me.

Who ordained us as the singers of praise,
off kilter on the stage, condemned, blissful,
and practiced, turning this world into the next
in a way, in a way that only we can imagine
and then not imagine?
Who designated our voices to sing for ourselves
and not ourselves, as if someone other than ourselves,
but also us, was listening? Just listening.
Who planted this bug inside us that picks up
everything we say and think,
then transmits it back to us in our sleep?
I'm tempted to say that without remembering my dreams
I could not sing.
Now for the price I pay for saying it.

I must be ready for the sight of her
in all her glory, steering the clouds of unknowing
with invisible reins, understanding
that history is double, both real and unreal,
both actual and mystical.

I must develop a potent weakness in the ruins
of my city, play both rough and merciful music.
Each face is a rebus of my own.
No one's born with a soul.
There's too much evidence to the contrary.
Too many voices crying out from stones.

No righteous man is better off than the wicked.
No one daddy less evil than another,
although we need to demonize one as the many.
To see ourselves as that connected.

I kick the glass in the street.
Gaze up to where the steeple was.
Kneel down to taste the dust at my feet.
How long can I wait
as the clouds pass over, erasing my face?

All this looking and still I can't detect
the actual edge-or is it a point?-
of your immaculate turning.
What consolation is all this fashion
that burns the seasons with short and long?
I lie with you on the shore, wrap
my head in the tides of your dress.
There, in the distance-dark-I see
the waters gather to an emptiness.

# DESCENT

I milked the smoke of my last cigarette
before I went with them, the beautiful
girls who came for me to take me down
across the river. Ordered me to remove
my clothes at each infernal floor,
and then my skin at the lowest level.

I saw you on a dock in Venice board
his yacht with the too unearthly name,
*Queen of Heaven*. We had dreamed
of sitting here at a table beneath
an umbrella, lilacs at the center,
resuming our quarrel about whether
the British had been immoral
in ending sati. You said they had.
I said they hadn't. We had dreamed
that the terrace of our cafe was also
a barge and we were floating around
the world from one great city to another.

You were beautiful in the way
you turned around to look at me.
I see you still in that position
of moving forward but looking back.

It seems strangely right in this bardo bar
where no one drinks that this occurred.
That we must lie to know the truth.
Go on speaking to someone in love to live again,
if only briefly, as I'm doing now.
To sing to you at the end about the lilacs.
How in their briefest bloom they last forever
on the tables in Venice. In the gardens of hell.

## THE BALIFF OF THE HEAVENLY COURT
## BRINGS GERRY TO THE LORD'S ATTENTION

Have you considered your servant Gerry,
How he races between one place and another.
He  is in awe of himself at 70.
How suddenly youthful and thin he looks!
He is flame on wheels, night on air,
crying to his beloved, "the skin of my soul
is soaked in oil and burns down the day."

He is savoring the breaks of light in the fog,
imagining real places on earth,
luminescent signs to turn around, turn around.
How long, he wonders, can I go on living
as such a healthy, afflicted man?

He is petitioning you from the roof
of a house in a storm, clutching a wire
in one hand and a turtle dove in the other.
He has grown devout in your disregard.

He is singing an old refrain as if it were new,
something he calls his secret song.
The eves are trembling as he sings
with newfound range. He is shocking
his children, boring the angels.

He claims you're in love with Gomer
the beautiful whore, which is why you knock
on  hotel doors and sing in banks and cause
such pain in righteous men.

He has acquired near perfect pitch
next to the chimney,
tuned himself with a broken fork.
"Death and death again," he sings

like the soul of a boy.
A mouth has grown in his side to accompany him.
He is a chorus unto himself.
His wasted body burns the dark, powerful in its bones.
He is a wealthy man with a few quarters
in his pocket and a stain on his shirt.

He has been tested now.
You've lost your bet.
He says it's not what you take away
that hurts in the end
but what you give,
as if he were you and not a man.
And this were heaven instead of earth.
And the buffalo chips had sunk instead of risen.
And one woman was not enough.

## THE GREATER VISION

One morning you rose from bed and stood
at the window with a broom in your hand,
gazing across the river. You were more beautiful
then than ever. I walked outside and studied
the water, how double it was as it flowed and stayed.
"By living now," I said, "we'll live forever.
We'll write our names across the water."
"No," you replied. "Something less that's also
greater called to me from the other side."
"You were," I said, "still suffering from a terrible fever."
"One of us, it whispered, must cross the river
in order to know its proper name. The one
who stays behind will speak it then as if its name
had always been. It will sit on your tongue,
or mine, like a little black bird and sing."

## ERROR AT THE HEART OF DESIRE

Where does she go around the corner?
Is it possible to know before I learn?
What do I see when she is there?
My eyes are useless at the sight of her.

*Here I am* on the street.
Send me over as a sacred mirror.
I am lost between her shape and form,
a shadow on Church and Pine.

I am a pool outside myself when she is near.
What does she see beneath my surface?
I am ignorant of the *objects* there,
the coins she has wished upon.

My love betrays a hidden stone.
I can not hold her in the rain.
I search for her like a river through hills
but cannot find her for long.

I see her only from a distance
where she is real, absorbed with strange details,
a lion's tooth and spinning wheel.
I guess her name to no avail.

I watch her fade into the air.
She disappears when I most want her.
I wait for her with the patience of water.
She comes to me with a terrible thirst.
I am quenched by the sight of her.
I am renewed by her lips upon my surface.

What can I say to interest her?
My lapping on the shore is not enough.

She is ignorant of those who most desire her.
I am mistaken about her nature.
What remains when she is gone?

How should I think in order to *know* her?
Where does she go beyond her form?
How does she stay when she is gone?

I have traveled the country
in search of her. The world is a blur
of peaks and valleys. Do I fly or walk?

I ask the trees to enlighten me.
I wash my eyes with rain.
Why do I think that time should cease
when I behold her?

There is an error at the heart of desire,
the thought of having her,
the thought that water puts out the flame.

I turn away for a while to clear my waters.
What do I see in her absence?
A toothless lion and pile of wool.
A temple floor and scattered straw.

She comes to me in my privation.
She sheds her dress to bathe in private.
It is dark where she swims from spring to spring.
I hold her there in liquid arms.
She bends the light of a million stars.

## IS SEX A SOILED GOWN

Is sex a soiled gown to throw away
or satin slip to wear beneath your skirt?
Reptilian suit for me that smells like hay

that's just been mowed on a summer day.
(Or is it the essence of harrowed dirt?)
Is sex a second skin to wash away

like a film of dust, residue of clay,
or natural salve to rub into the hurt,
a sweet, addictive sweat that smells like hay.

We are so quick to bathe and then betray
our scent with oils and musk, to purge our shirts.
Is sex a shameful smell to wash away

or keep as a sign of us, as if to say,
*Oh shame, mother of fashion, please convert?*
This tight reptilian suit that smells like hay

was the suit I wore the night I went astray.
I put it on again like an old pervert.
It is the evening wear I wear all day,
this slick reptilian suit that smells like hay.

# A GLIMPSE OF THE AFTERLIFE

I'm smoking a cigarette and having a drink
with my gazelle at the Empyreal Grill and Bar.
I'm telling her a joke that isn't that funny
but we laugh anyway as if it were,
and then it is. Ideal forms are every-
where, the chairs on which we sit, the windows
to our left and right, our risen bodies
at the perfect table. It's my idea of heaven
to be with her on earth, breathing the air
in a smoke-filled room, drinking tonic
laced with gin, listening to the king.
The conversation rises to a deeper level.
She disagrees with me again on a matter
of religion, as if religion still mattered
in the afterlife, as if there were
no greater joy than talking to the one
you love about an idea you had in life.
I'm drawn to her in direct proportion to
the differences of our opinions, ecstatic
to find our bodies have survived in heaven.
There is also time in the eternal evening
as the darkness thickens. I retrieve her shawl
from the back of her chair and cover her shoulders
which have begun to shiver in the chill
of heaven. I have passed from one plane to the next
without detecting the slightest change, except
I know my body lies somewhere beneath
the dirt I walk on now as we leave the bar.
I know the greatest mercy of all in the end
is to be with the one you love beneath
a sky on which it's written: You have died
ten thousand times and you will die again.

# THE BOOK OF DARKNESS

I picked up the book of darkness from off
the ground and began to read each page,
the chapter on shadows, the chapter on caves.
I thought about nothing and being in it.
I thought the stars were notes for a dream's live music.
I sat in the dark and thought the sky was full of music.
Read each day revised by night as the same bright script
as the day before with only the slightest difference.
I wrote this difference in the dirt with a sharp
dead stick: the infinite minute sooner it took
the sun to set, the always variable
New England text, the news of the day
that I forget. I sat among the books
of evening, listening to the pages turn above.
So quickly read, so incomprehensible.
I lay like a locust beneath the covers both
black and blank as the sun went under
and all there was was the darkness *her hand* uncovered.

## THE BELLE OF AMHERST

After kissing death on the mouth
you grew immensely beautiful but cold
to the suitors who left their cards.
Too often the same uxorious colonel in disguise,
handsome but callow, a victim of peace,
no scar on his thigh or death in his eye,
had proposed to you in uniform.
The kiss had given you strength to resist.
To write yourself in all your *possible sublimity*.
Aboriginal and white. A sustenance.

"I cannot live with You-"
she wrote her Master.
"It would be Life-
and Life is over there-"
You were both vague and specific about the place,
as if the place, "behind the shelf,"
were death in life, no *cold rising vast*
to stir your soul, preserve the terror.

The loss instilled your eyes with a sight
that pierced the darkness, a sadness.
You grew widely famous as the Belle of Amherst
who gardened at night.
Who covered your yard with stones,
as if your ground, rife with flowers,
were a grave for all your hearts beneath.

## THE RAIN AS RAIN

I have made a career of lying about the world.
I thought it was what people wanted to hear,
that love, for instance, was a pomegranate
and death just another animal.
I'm no longer in the mood for religious poetry.
I've received a commission from the sky to study rain.
It's a high commission.
No turning the drops into something else.
No restlessness with the way things are
because suddenly everything is enough on its own.
No matter how hard I try
it's impossible to find a metaphor for the rain
that's falling in the yard and on the house.
You know what it sounds and feels like already
without any help from me.
But what is it exactly when you're this clear
about the world and the steady downfall
is more an accompaniment to what you're thinking about?
How can I tell you without telling you
that rain is its own metaphor, always something else
than what it is, as well as the same.
How do I say rain in other words and convey
at the same time that it isn't raining the same rain
then when I wasn't thinking about the rain?
When I was simply taking it in
as a particular of a particular day
and remember it now in this rain as that other rain
that fell and fell and fell?

# JUDITH

I dropped my rifle in the midst of war and followed you
to the desert where each morning the first thing I saw
was a murder of crows picking at the bones of your dead mules.
What was I thinking? That there was still a way to relish
the taste of a golden apple and live with you in paradise?

You were so beautiful the entire army of Holofernes
turned their heads when you walked by and thought,
"There is no woman like her from one end of the earth
to the other, so lovely of face and wise of speech. "

There was too much dream in your eyes for me to think
about tomorrow, something in your smile that called me back
to the beginning when I thought in terms of forever.
What was I thinking? That Nebuchadnezzar had surrendered?
That Antiochus had repented? That the fatwa had been lifted?

Every day with you was a sandy existence of paradise
and oblivion. Why Gilgamesh left Siduri at the bar.
Why Odysseus left Calypso on her shore. Too much Sahara
in the end, beautiful as you were, my infinite woman rolling
over in bed, shifting in the wind, drawing me in.

What was I thinking? That form was enough as long
as it changed while remaining the same?
What else could lure me away from my men before the battle?
What else could cause me to think that it was possible
to live on thought alone but thought itself?

My mind was on fire with the light blue flame of a dream,
the thought that you were Queen of Heaven and I the King,
and as long as I burned I'd live forever.
The thought was housed in the flame.
The flame was stolen from heaven.

What was I thinking? That I was dead already?
That alive? That I could live as smoke for a while
then disappear, elope with you in the high desert air?

# ACHERON

I arrived at the bank to find
you already there on the opposite side,
failing at names for the sullen flow.

I lay beneath the willows with a violent passion,
but kept it to myself, grew quickly older.
Years were days.

You stared at the passing mirror,
then dipped your hair beneath the surface.
The older man beside you said,

"This is the end of beauty."
"I am the same," you cried.
"The water has changed."

"The water has moved," he said,
"and you have died. I saw your fear
become desire on the other side."

You sang a song about a mountain range
and uncut grass and spider web
across the void you called your path.

We cast for fish with shining lines
and spoke like friends about the weather,
still the same. You caught a trout

and threw him back for lack of hunger.
Their bites were frequent there,
despite the days our lines were lingered.

I was abused by the ferryman for being alive
and fell like lightening across the river.
I was a leaf inside the thunder.

# WINTER ROSES

I was so weary of the world.
I was so sick of it.

D.H. LAWRENCE

1

*I crossed over into another world*
like a frightened child who wishes to go.
I was very glad, *and all alone in the world.*
I trespassed into the unknown,
welcome and joyous with sorrow,
reborn in the labor of winter days.
I called it the kingdom of heaven within me.
I practiced form for speaking plain.

*I cried with joy, because I was in the new world,*
*just ventured in.*

I was not what I seemed, volatile form,
bright flame at night, tiger in the veldt.
I had not survived but died
and then awakened from the dream of death.
I was the willing body of death, starved in my grave.

2

There is only one lesson for those who grieve,
*no change of heart or spiritual conversion.*
The wind never returns to review its breeze.
The river flows intractably.
This is the blessing. Remorseless urgency.

Hard stare of sky. I was rearranged in bliss
to believe that energy itself is sacred,
creating the world. Judging the world.
Everything passes into nothing and only this moment
is real but gone, both redeemed and destroyed
in a perfect but harsh religion.
A green eyed woman blinded me in the clear.
I buried her in the air and lost my way.
She was beloved, leading behind.
Singing to me this very song.
The sweep and settle of sacred dust
concealed my steps, christened the past.


3

I repeated in a flood of sunshine,
"This is a dark place. This is a dark place."
I washed my eyes with paint,
stuffed my ears with dirt.

I felt a joy beyond the joy I used to sing.
My soul that wasn't a soul had died
and left me there where I was dumb
and wished to feel the very thing I could not feel
and continue to live.

I sat like a crow on top of the barn
and saw how mean my love had grown,
how many bodies lay dead in the fields
from all my killing, pile upon pile.
I had become a murderer from loving,
and this was good, very good.
I was a stranger among friends in this unknown,

too familiar husband to the woman I loved.
I hung my eyes in blindness from the sky
and beckoned to the clouds, "Take your revenge.
I thought I was alive because of them."


4

I held my wife at night to find myself,
touched her back and thighs.
She said, "There you are in her sleep,"
but I was awake and there but not there.
I was as I told her, ready to die.
I rubbed her body and made a wish
to be reborn, to die to all these nights
of living in the old world, to step
onto the raft of death and float along,
float along, to sleep like this beneath
the sky, stirring in the morning of my demise,
flinging out my hand like the hand
of a soul onto the shore, onto her side,
rise up renewed, awake and mad,
unable to describe what I saw.
No, utterly in awe, standing alone,
joyous with life, ready to dance.


5

A man approached me who was I
from across the field that was every field
I had ever been in.
Held up a stick and stared at me.
This was not a dream but a way of seeing without my eyes.
I had died and this was good.

I had killed everything with my eyes,
poisoned the world with myself.
Deceived myself with names: sky, trees, flowers, birds.
As if name alone could protect a thing as other.
As if names alone could free the world from me.

I helped myself up from off the ground
that was now unknown and walked the earth
With defiant knowledge, planted roses in winter.


6

I had a vision of the Missouri inside my heart,
as if I were America itself, split in the middle
by a dirty river, while the lone citizen
I called my spirit wandered naked on the shore,
straining on the fog to catch a glimpse
of my beloved on the other side,
although I saw nothing except that water running
into the wider river, sweeping along with terrible
force, slow as it was, filling the sky.

## PASTERNAK

*What century have we got out there, my dears?*

BORIS PASTERNAK

This was the life, to live in Russia
at the end of Russia and write about its history
as if it were poetry, while one beloved or the other
lay asleep nearby, dreaming of him writing nearby
in a high-ceilinged room with the vista
of snow-covered mountains, forests and fields.
More ice than glass in the window frames.
A red coal in the samovar.
Outside, in the distance, the endless rain
of shells and sough of trains behind the hills.
The old world falling to its knees like an elephant.

This was the life, to live at Peredelkino
like a prophet in his own land and dream.
"What I have lost is much too great for a single man,"
he writes in the snow with the tip of his cane.
The shelling has stopped and the world has changed.
The wind picks up and blows the words away.
He writes for the eyes that follow him,
"Nothing is lost in the other world."
This dark December day inspires him to write
the plainest things in the snow, then walk away.

# EPITAPH

Knowledge made its bloody entry.

A black hat sat on my heart.

Language lived in an unmarked box.

An old man, on a plane, years later,
turned and said to me:

*The dead are buried in us alive.*
*The future is the past on tragic days.*

Maybe it was a train.

# REVIVAL

I went under to repent in the dark
of her Sunday dress. I worked as I went,
removing the antimacassars.
I was of the faith that posited elbows
against the grain of native oak,
knees on the veins of mountain granite.
I spoke in tongues with arms outstretched.
She wrote it down, then ripped it up.
A cloud of witnesses sang amen.
I was ready then to perform a miracle.
Candles flickered against the stone.
Incense burned inside the thurible.
There was a choir of unchanged voices
and Latin text. She shrove me stripped
before the altar. The Spirit entered me
like a pawl in a ratchet wheel to keep
my mind from falling back to her.
"Take, eat," she said. "This is my body."
There was a table spread beneath the crucifix.
I rose with the light inside my mouth
and swallowed it. I thought of it.
I thought of it! The windows cracked.
Arches fell. I left her there, converted.

# FLIGHT DELAY AT TERMINAL X

The double voice of a woman speaks from above
announcing times, gates and caveats, while also
declaring, "Walk like a man in the eschaton.
Carry your carry on as if nothing were inside."
The jet engines' roar outside is the sound I need
to imagine the force beyond the liftoffs of routine
flights: the iron legs of Mr. Ant, the thirst of cork
in March, the worker bee's ballet. Only the din
of disparate voices fills the air of Terminal X.
I am alone in this concourse, immune at last
to the babe in damask who cannot speak.
Immune to the crowds that are and are not there.
That close to a bardo state as I stare outside
at the loud indignant birds and conjure
a cynosure in their midst beckoning me
from the tarmac to rise from my chair and join
her there beneath the wings, in the wind of planes.
To walk hand in hand down the runway as if
it were water, reciting the analects that matter most,
preparing, as it were, for the worst, with truths
on our lips, keeping our distance while nonetheless
touching, giving up our seats in bliss to the standbys.
She is the one whose voice bedights the air
in the concourse, who must be conjured first
before she is recognized in her peasant dress,
someone you've known before, but not like this.
There now, in mufti, shining like Laura,
she espouses the law on the runway under
the duress of the irate man for whom this pilgrimage
is slow per force, for whom she waits in the median
within *a cloud of flowers*. What was I waiting for

that wasn't here already? This delay is a blessing,
therefore, for anyone who hears, which is, to see.
How to stay in that domain where you belong,
but is not home? How to explain? *I saw the angel
who was not there but spoke to me from the other world
that was also here, whom I imagined and then proclaimed.*
All the planes that I have missed in the meantime
are testaments *to my delay.* "Let them land without
me ," I say to the guard who comes for me in my chair
that is perfect, where all I feel is the grip of her hand.